T0146940

PHOENIX FEATHERS

KRISTINA GOLTSIS

BALBOA.
PRESS

A DIVISION OF HAY HOUSE

Balboa Press books may be ordered through booksellers or by contacting:

Balboa Press
A Division of Hay House
1663 Liberty Drive
Bloomington, IN 47403
www.balboapress.com
1 (877) 407-4847

Because of the dynamic nature of the Internet, any web addresses or
links contained in this book may have changed since publication and
may no longer be valid. The views expressed in this work are solely those
of the author and do not necessarily reflect the views of the publisher,
and the publisher hereby disclaims any responsibility for them.

The author of this book does not dispense medical advice or prescribe
the use of any technique as a form of treatment for physical, emotional,
or medical problems without the advice of a physician, either directly
or indirectly. The intent of the author is only to offer information
of a general nature to help you in your quest for emotional and
spiritual well-being. In the event you use any of the information in
this book for yourself, which is your constitutional right, the author
and the publisher assume no responsibility for your actions.

Any people depicted in stock imagery provided by Thinkstock are
models, and such images are being used for illustrative purposes only.
Certain stock imagery © Thinkstock.

Print information available on the last page.

ISBN: 978-1-5043-8883-2 (sc)
ISBN: 978-1-5043-8885-6 (hc)
ISBN: 978-1-5043-8884-9 (e)

Library of Congress Control Number: 2017914729

Balboa Press rev. date: 09/26/2017

Adam,

Thank you for letting me burn in order to help me rise.
Thank you for setting me on fire all over again, ever since.

I love you.

"A heart filled with love is like a phoenix
that no cage can imprison"

- Rumi

Contents

chapter one
γέννηση; gennisi; birth

chapter two
θάνατος; thanatos; death

chapter three
ανάσταση; anastasi; resurrection

Preface

Phoenix Feathers is a story about survival. After years of saving written work under folders titled "stress writing", I began to acknowledge that the art of creative expression had become my only method of true relaxation. As a young woman with depression & anxiety, I had chosen to confront my experiences with conscious reflection & mindful intention by documenting my thoughts through poetry.

Read as a fragmented stream of consciousness, Phoenix Feathers is a story of how I saved my own life. I hope it will offer nourishment to yours as well.

Acknowledgements

To my beautiful grandparents, Tom & Vera – for taking me in & raising me like a daughter. For your incredible patience, your lessons of resilience, your morals, your kefi & your love.

To my wonderful parents, Peter & Irene – for helping me grow into a woman. For trusting my choices. For drying my tears. For the tough love. For the unconditional love. For everything.

My darling sister, Stacey – for enduring my darkest hours & always loving me anyways. For being my partner in crime. For helping me edit this entire project without rolling your eyes. For believing in me. (It will always be you & me, coco.)

To my Godmother Julia for insisting that I write since I was a child. To my cousin, Thomas for flying to Florida with me in support of my writing dreams. To Vanessa for fueling my creative fires & pushing me out of my comfort zone. To Summer for your overwhelming sisterhood & refusing to ever let me fall.

To my sweetheart, Adam – For being the catalyst of my artistic awakening. For manifesting our dreams. For trusting my choices & taking risks. For everything that you are, & all that you have inspired me to become.

To those who have taken the time to read my work. To those with fires in your chests.

Thank you.
I love you.

Introduction

Beloved Human,

The purpose of this poetry collection is to gift your soul with comfort.

I hope to re-affirm your belief that the universe will always align with intention & that every phase of your life will be fueled with beauty & wisdom if you know where to look. Honour the innocence, chaos & reincarnation of your existence as cherished heirlooms. Know that every moment of defeat offers an opportunity for a new beginning, & if you choose to rise from the bitter ashes, you will always discover that you can fly.

With love,
Kristina

chapter one
γέννηση; gennisi; birth

I would like to think of birth
as the mystical bi-product
to a cosmic spectacle;

The conception of life,
the formation of our universe,
the birth of a phoenix.

But all forms of matter
exist within the realm
of the fantastic

All it takes is a willing eye
to deconstruct existence
with love.

- look harder

Youth is not an age. Instead, it is a commitment to embracing joy, humour & opportunity. It is smiling when you have permission to cry & crying when you feel that you need to. It is knowing that there are great moments to come & being openly eager to receiving them. It is waiting for something spectacular to happen. It is making spectacular things happen.

- I plan to live forever

If truth is what you're seeking,
rise up & follow me.
I know a place where dreams are made,
where rivers meet the sea.

You raise a brow to question
why there's not a soul in sight...
but listen child, you see this view
belongs to you each night.

This bench on which we're resting
exists within your mind
so that you could contemplate great things
like the value of being kind.

In silence, tossing pebbles
bouncing slow across the sea
I watched your eyes fill up with love
as you realized what this means!

The truth that you were seeking
was within you all along
& all that contradicts your heart
turned out to be all wrong.

Now promise, every evening
while you're drifting off to sleep
you'll find your way back to this place
to share your truths with me.

- unexpected strangers

A tree is not plucked from its roots
to be admired for its natural beauty.

Let people grow wild, too.

- *clarity beneath the clouds*

I, like you
twist beneath the stars.
Plunging deep below the depths of consciousness
with outstretched palms,
we howl to the moon.

- we are all a part of something greater

I am most curious about
what blooms in your darkness.
What sets flames to your heart
when your mind will not wake?
What seed has been planted
in the core of your being
that defines the great journey
you were brought here to take?

Will our fates cross
just like planes in the clouds
& will you still be here
when the turbulence break?

Despite paths of our futures
please keep your hearts open
& fight to keep dreaming
even when you're awake.

- who are you when you're alone?

I am the living,
breathing, reincarnation
of my ancestry.

With a heart committed
to the dance of Piraeus,
the weathered pillars of my
persistent ψυχή*
refuse to crumble
beneath the weight
of philosophical
apathy.

- my bones are like home

* ψυχή = soul

What is your greatest fear?
Vulnerability.

What is your greatest affection?
Vulnerability.

- the interview

Ascend in slumber
to the place where peace resides.
Return as needed.

- where is your happy place?

Find me amidst your darkest corners
where we can create light from nothing

Isn't that why we exist?
Because God felt so deeply that his love exploded?

- I have so many questions

Tilt your eager mouths to the sun.
Swallow a mouthful of sunshine
to warm your gentle face.

It is you who yearns for beauty,
it is you who yearns for light!

Seek hope in all dark places
& bloom despite
the fight.

- learning how to grow

Affirm your brilliance
through the peaks of your curves
with the valleys of space
that expose them.

Small, gentle beings
wrapped up in soft earth
give thanks to the riches
you came in.

- we are of the same soil

All the dreams we have yet to chase
full of road maps to victories
demanding that we follow.

- we are always at a fork in the road

phoenix feathers

Beware the stagnant comfort zone
that binds you to the floor;
restricting you between the lines
despite your need for more.

Do not stay here any longer
than you need to, if you must!
A leap of faith will set you free
but only if you trust!

- *limits do not exist*

Though I'm sure God sprinkled stardust
in the creation of your eyes,
I pray that when mine meet your gaze
your suns & moons collide.

- how do I make you feel?

Scattered white petals
embellishing our daydreams
Love me, love me not.

- I think I'm starting to feel something

Capture me within the lines & shades
that cascade around your aura
each time we are near.

Paint me in strokes that
highlight the peaks & valleys
with familiar paths,
inviting you in.

I am home within my bones,
but you are always welcome
for the steamiest cups
of tea.

- kindly rsvp

Your soul has a freshness
like cool, fresh linens on a warm summer day
wrapped up in pale surfaces of embroidered fabric,
you coax me to stay.

The corners will lift like
warped mosses, & your limbs
line mine like garden rows

How gentle the brush of your skin against mine
like waves embraced by ocean foam.

- ocean foam

Trust my honest words
& should the risk deter you
trust my body, too.

- learning how to love

phoenix feathers

There is something about you
that stirs chaos inside of me
I lay wide awake each night
adorned in gentle smiles

The breath of spring inspires
my skin to grasp your honest gaze
& I find myself with
thoughts of you
for days.

- there was something in the air that day

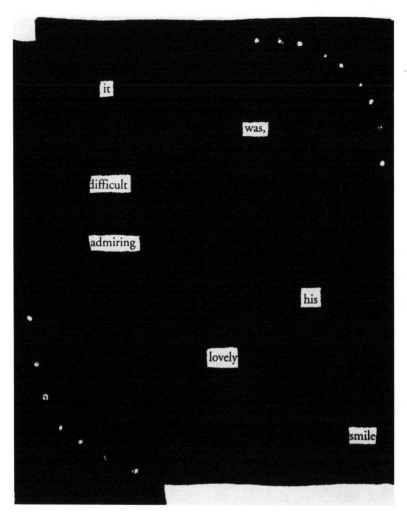

- it was difficult admiring his lovely smile

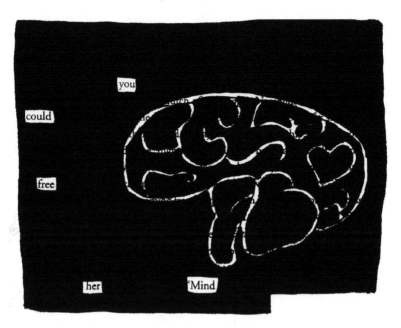

- you could free her mind

There is a fortress of peace
nestled deep within the crook
of your neck.

Your groggy morning eyes
are like the sun.

Each tight embrace persuades
my sprouting limbs to anchor roots
so that your sly, gentle lips
become my
moat.

- the first

I was a shadow before you arrived.
Sheltered from the warm, plush blankets
of your cool summer skies;
I waited patiently to tumble with the tides.
Floating still, so that I might learn the
constellations to every star within
your
eyes.

- *the things we'd whisper*

Didn't you know that I was
a warrior,
love?

The battle was over
when you surrendered to
me.

- love & war

I can still recall the position of
every last goose bump that had danced
upon your skin. Each one parallel to
the fireworks & earthquakes that filled up
behind my eyes the moment they found
rest upon your
smile.

- you create the most wonderful chaos inside of me

Only you can make
silence sing like wild birds.
Oh, how you free me.

- *bpm*

Love like this
does not exist in most imaginations,
but we have never belonged to the
binding planes that steady
our humble
feet.

- freedom seekers

You must be other-worldly
the way you imitate the sun.
With burning eyes, you warm my skin
even when the day is done.

I absorb your rays, like magic,
suspended in thin air.
I can close my eyes, fill up my lungs
& trust that you'll be there.

So, should the moon fall from the sky
I would not weep a tear,
for that which illuminates the dark
will always be right here.

- I am no longer afraid

There is a place in my mouth reserved for you
guarded by these brittle teeth.
Below the palate & above the tongue
of memories, bitter-sweet.

Despite the decay of cool aged flesh,
below the soils of our retreat;
Right here, the proof of you lays rest
long after my heart's defeat.

- *eternal*

Love seals in me
every hope.
If I am made of clouds,
then they have cleared to blue.

A sea of shallow water,
I am safe beside the sun.

- Helios

There are diamonds
in my bones
that only sparkle
when you belong
to
me.

- *love over diamonds*

I fell in love with your dialect
without hearing a word you've said.

But there is a language to your movements;
each twist a foreign prompt to
make me
beg.

- *body language*

Fade to shades of crimson
while we navigate the dark
invite the heat to rise
& light the way.

Pour bottles into cups
I seem to have been here before.
Yet somehow now,
my knees have melted
into clay...

- in the palm of your hands

Our words had run dry
but our bodies left soaking
making waves each night.

- naughtical

Your lips were like ripe berries
gushing of fragrant wine
& I find myself intoxicated by the thought
of your lavish flavours
spilling freely down my
spine.

How rich the taste of urgency
upon your eager tongue
with eyes full of the spectacle
before you.

Admire my curves as artifacts
comprised of cosmic dust;
with dips & swells that
burn beneath the tension
of your touch.

Melt into vulgar memories
that emerge within your sheets;
before, behind, between
below, beneath.

I feel most alive when the moon hangs full
against the black, velvet sky
with your eyes devouring me
like hungry
wolves...

- *wanted*

Perhaps angels count our street lamps at night in order to fall asleep. Creating stories of meaning from the constellations of our cities, gazing down in awe.

Perhaps they make wishes upon the pale, blinking lights of drifting planes, staring fragments of hope into the Statue of Liberty's serene, unblinking eyes.

I hope they pray for us, too.
However, how many of us have been praying for them?

- drowsy contemplation

If tomorrow fails to come,
just know that I have roamed this earth
with love in my footprints,
hope in my heart,
& passion in my bones.

- this is how I would like to be remembered

Perhaps we are too young.

With wisps of silver dancing in our hair alongside the valleys of memories outlining our skin,
are we far too young to comprehend the fires burning in the hollows of our chests? Are we too young to make sense of this complicated simplicity, despite the cyclical reality of it all? My ears are as underdeveloped as my eyes in observation. Please, teach me to see?

I beg you to sing me your silence. Only then can I learn to grow & evolve.
Are we too young to trust entirely?
Is that why we suffocate within the webs of our fears?
Is it true that you will cover me like the sea & free me of my demons?

With outstretched arms, I offer myself to your will.
Hold me within the palm of your hand & I will surrender.
Fill me with a love that I will only begin to understand long after my bones have turned to dust, & I will promise to search for your unspoken truths.

When you release me of my restraints, I will rise above the clouds & celebrate these milestones hidden within the proud glint of your watchful eye. Towards the sun, I will accept my enlightened freedom with relief, honour & gratitude.

But for now, maybe we are just far too young to understand.

- trying to make sense of things

chapter two
θάνατος; thanatos; death

"It hurts"
I said
to my oversized heart
"I know"
it said
"I'm sorry"

- *perhaps bigger is not always better*

There are days where words
float off my tongue like paper lanterns,
illuminating the sky with gentle grace.
& there are days where my words
are swallowed whole, caged behind the
prison of my apathetic teeth.

Today is one of those days.

- the entire spectrum

Let me think upon the feeling
of your chest pressed up to mine.
Affirm the beating heart that still resides.
Watch the traces of our pasts
that seem to age through many moons
dissolving through the vacancies
of time.

- I can feel you slipping away

So fleeting, those moments on the wall.
Senseless hands consuming moments
from which we thrive;
new life,
new love,
death.

Memories that inspire, seduce, & tick, tick, tick us off
summed up by no extraordinary depiction
than two metal hands
stretched outwardly
in opposite directions.

- running out of time

There are days where I feel lonely,
& there are days where I'd just rather
be alone.

These are not the same kind of days.

- understanding solitude

There are thorns in my throat
from all of the secrets we've buried
& they keep getting harder
to swallow.

- roses & lie lilies

Searching through rivers
will never compare to the
tides of his ocean.

- undertow

Lying next to you in the dark,
we contrast the dreams & visions of a future
that you could never offer.

Fingers interlaced,
you breathe reminders to be present
into the skin on my neck
creating wishes upon the goosebumps that arise.

- fighting the inevitable

I've sewn white feathers to your
pillows each time you leave because
they feel like your eyelashes pressed
against my cheek.

I've poured fresh rainwater
down the stairs to cleanse & praise
your tired feet
I've coaxed the sun to dim the skies
& share the stars to
help you rest

Yet somehow still, my darling dear,
I'm still alone.

- with love, heartbreak

Consume me. Consume all of me.
What good is that in which does not serve to nourish?
Breathe me in deeply in that I might visit the nearest points
to your heart.

Does it still beat for me? A subtle, but promising rhythm
undeniable in its persistence?
I've chosen to dwell within the parts of you that hunger for
solace.

Please.
Let me in.

- I don't want to lose you

There are traumas in my spine
from bullet holes refusing to heal.

Pouring out, eternally
like grapes cured by time
into the finest wines to ever
meet the palate.

- pouring myself dry

"Melancholy" is such a pretty word to describe this
tropical storm.
To feel pensive & sad beneath the rains of transition...
Let us wrap our arms around one another,
& sigh.

This sadness is such a necessary season.
Just like the trees, we are so lovely when
we set the dead parts of ourselves
free.

- abscission

Whiskey burns my tongue
while I burn your photographs
until I forget.

- the ritual

My prison cell has a welcome mat,
but I haven't any guests.
The gates unlocked, but I stay here
so my tired limbs might rest.
The kettle's on with mugs for two,
but one always gets cold.
I tried to host a poker game
but I'm always forced to fold.
Perhaps you'd like a movie night?
Or some silent meditation?
I hate the void but it's all I find
with social isolation.

So, I'll wait here with a bright, sad smile
& paint the walls with blue
for in case one day you do drop by
(& I really hope you do).

- madness leads to tea parties

I spun violently in circles confronted by hundreds of versions of myself collected before my eyes. With my heart in my throat & a knife in my hand, I became dizzied by the sea of faces staring back at me with haunting eyes. Maddened by my inability to decipher the threatening from the nonthreatening, I let my eyes sweep across their identical faces as my intuition whispered words of recognition through my thoughts: greedy, powerful, fearless, generous, murderous, lustful, resilient, defeated...

Hundreds of copies mirroring me with intrusive eyes. Each one personified by each human characteristic I have ever once embodied. Why was it so difficult to decide which ones should survive?

It is terrifying to realize that the kind & innocent masks we wear do not ensure that we are good people. There is a yin & a yang inside each of us. Some poisonous vermin that stretches its tired limbs in awakening each time your voice of reason falls weak.

Scattered echoes in protest rung through the air as the faces grew nearer. Suppress your demons, deny them!

Frantic & afraid, I killed all but one before I left. Problem is, I could never tell which one it was that survive... I guess that's the risk we take with a pretty face.

- deceit

There is a hell in my head threatened by the small glimpses of heaven that I keep finding in people. The way their smiles make my knees weak & my foolish heart is always falling in love. But my mind never fails to conquer, fists flailing in a burning blaze to build walls around my loneliness to remind me to trust nothing that doesn't hurt. I am most alive when I'm burning, you see?

Love isn't a real thing. How can it be when it is created from the same chemicals that are released by eating chocolate? Devil's food cake is no coincidence, my dear. Bury your naivety under the blankets that deceive you. There is a reason that heartbreak sparks so much creativity.

There is no questioning pain.

- fondue

I hid your blood within my own veins to protect you; battling the skeletons in your closet with my bare hands. Bonnie & Clyde, you would tell me with a charismatic smile intended to melt my heart into my thighs. Even the smartest of women crumble at the mercy of a full heart. (even a black, soulless one)

How proudly I would hang your medals of dishonesty & infidelity alongside my hard-earned degrees. Pieces of paper that I had invested years' worth of tears, stress & sleepless nights all for a better future. Scraps of paper that I would have willingly set on fire had you needed to keep warm.

Foolish girl. We are all addicted to love, aren't we? Or are we addicted to avoiding our own insecurities & loneliness? What have you done for love? What would you do for love? & what happens when it's over, my darling? Would you die a thousand deaths where only more pain could bring some relief & pleasure?

Please, stay quiet while I listen to the voices of our poison.

We are all psychotic.

Fetch me your shovel, my love. I would never let you dig our graves alone.

- *grave diggers*

I have
tried to
avoid things
that remind
me of
you,
but I cannot
seem
to shed
my
skin.

- coping mechanisms

Coffee rings on the night stand.
Darkness.
Crumpled photos on the floor.
I wait.

I mistake the sounds of settling
walls for footsteps down the hall,
& I sense a hint of lust
crawl down my spine.

"I knew you would be back",
I welcomed Death with open arms.
"Each time you come too close
is such a thrill"

The hooded cloak exhaled a
stream of smoke through grinning lips;

"For a chance to feel alive?
Some folks would
kill".

- *cynical & caffeinated*

My skin holds the sounds
of muffled words held captive
since your eager teeth.

- keep quiet

There you are, my bright little rosebush.
Struggling to blossom against autumns cruel chill.
Seeping through my open windows, you fill the room with
your fragrance.

Planted in the darkest part of my soul,
hiding the bones of buried demons beneath your soil.
My hands are bloody from holding on too tight as you
taunt me.

Drunk off hope, swimming in a bottomless sea;
why won't it ever stop raining?

- September rain

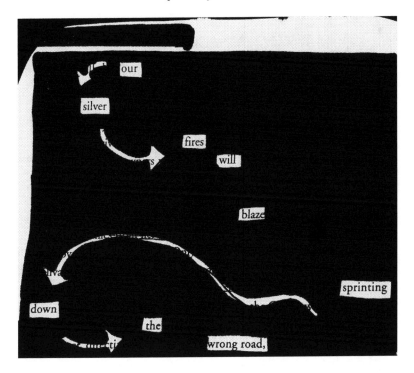

- our silver fires will blaze sprinting down the wrong road

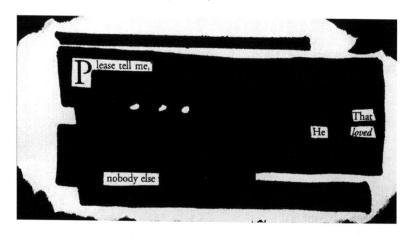

- please tell me that he loved nobody else

phoenix feathers

You wore my lipstick stains like battle paint
etched into your skin like wine colored photographs.
You can't build a home on false promises, you know?
the foundation always sunk too soon.

The bartenders on the southwest side of Brooklyn
seem to sink through more exit signs than welcomes
hunting for lipstick marked whiskey glasses...

Pour yourself a drink instead, love
It's just as good for tearing open
old wounds.

- wasted on the rocks

It must be true – I'm doomed, you see.
The lesser half of humanity.
The one who risks irrelevance unless
someone's consuming me.

A waste of time it was, indeed.
Dollars spent on school degrees
to hang on walls, collecting dust
while I'm advised to look pretty.

"Be seen, not heard" they'd say to me
while stripping away my dignity
to make room for sexual displays
hoping someone might finance me.

"Don't be too smart, just be carefree!
'cause no one likes a strong lady
that makes her man look like a fool
despite inferiority"

So hand me the perfume now, please
to mask the stench of atrocities
while you zip up the body bag
of all I would have liked to be.

- *cause of death: vanity*

Did you think you were complimenting her when she poured herself into your meal? Praising her for a neatly kept home? The women we silence for their ability to be self-sufficient is not a reflection of "wife-material" but rather a reflection of your expectations in a partnership. Instead, thank her for her resilience, imagination or drive. Loneliness should not exist in team work. If it does, you're doing it wrong.

- enough

Hostile creature, adorned in false jewels
did you not know that respect should be earned?

Kill off your arrogance & re-learn your place
before your empire crumbles
& burns.

- the blunder of false idols

It frustrates me
that the same brain
that once reigned in
the creation of serotonin
has since flipped production
to cortisol & won't listen
to me when I insist that
this was a terrible
business decision.

- losing my mind

I do not write poetry.
I purge.

- *confessions*

I must be worth more
than heartache after heartache
please, tell me there's more.

- cheque, please

We are better off trusting our livers
as opposed to our fickle hearts.

At least they're always trying
to force all of the poison
out.

- anatomy of healing

Why do we desecrate our energy to the worship of destruction? Despite the flames that lay dormant within the cradles of our ribs & the knowledge that warmth is what welds together our brokenness? Why must we burn each other instead, constructing walls around our willingness? Who hurt you enough to confuse you? Who hurt you enough to turn you cold?

- it feels like the world is burning

We are mirrored by desolate dichotomies
that heighten the deafening silence
Rain-drummed windowsills mask the wreaths of ruins
that pour loosely from our eyes.

What's left to fight for on deserted land?
Home of the free? United we stand?

Systems crack concealing the cruelty of concrete craniums
struggling to process the persistence of social paralysis.
What must happen now?

The stairway to heaven was shorter than promised
& in its place, a labyrinth hell.
Leave your bags in my cardiac chambers, now.
You see, united we fall.

- our differences are only man-made

I'll climb these blood-stained mountain tops
with eager calloused hands
to say a prayer for all the dreams
abandoned in the sands.

One thousand burning candles
will illuminate the way,
lining paths of memories
as night shifts into day.

The only finite death is in
the threat of giving up!
Our numbered days unsure of when
these fires might erupt.

So, should this molten rubble
turn itself to roads that save
& all our hushed confessions
escape from silenced graves
we would rise like twin-flame lovers
preserved in old Pompeii
leaving traces of our victories
while cherubs guide the way.

So when the sun does set again
upon this ancient land,
let whispers murmur through the breeze
provoked by wanting hands.
Our warm embrace solidified
by Rome's mythology
& our hopeful limbs a reference for
sacred geometry.
The steady hum of trumpets
will fuel dawn's persistent waking,
exuding rays that kiss the earth

with what's ours for the taking!
We will rest here beneath the dust
that's settled in the sea,
claiming our home as watchful eyes
for all eternity.

- artifacts of what could have been

I am a fortress
with wide brass doors,
sheltering you from your demons.
Constructed in solitude,
I serve to protect.

I am a moat
separating myself from the stability of your promised lands
isolating this space of freedom
to which you freely seek comfort.

I hold you within my stone walls,
collecting your secrets within the notes of
our moonlit dance.
& so, in return for an echo in the silence;
I offer you solace
I offer you sanctuary
I offer you hope.

But when the sun awakens, I will draw back my bridges
releasing you into your reality
retaining the fragments of myself that long to follow
you out.

I stand alone.

Hidden beneath the cool rains of my personal storm,
I am cleansed & abandoned
Eroding the soil further & further away
from the bridges that unite us.

- I am a fortress

Maybe I am addicted to vulnerability.
The way that it cuts me & sews me,
lifts me, then molds me...

What an experience it is to gain access
to another's intangible soul.

People are so beautiful when they're raw.

- untreatable

We do not need to move
in the same direction
to be moving forward.

Like two ships passing voyage
parallel across the sea-
smiling silently into their
watery reflections cast by
the lonely lunar
moon.

No words need be spoken
to acknowledge a humble respect
between two lovers become
friends.

The past remains in memories
clutched tightly to my chest-
as the waves exchange a tide
of slow goodbyes.

- voyagers

There are days that feel like poetry
& days that feel like grief
But my, how grand the spectacle
each time these lovers meet.

- collide

What were you like, before fear set in?
I bet your laugh was incredible.
In fact, I bet it would shake the walls of your ribcage into symphonies of joy.

I bet you felt beautiful, too.
Free from the constraint of manufactured fabrics,
parading God's green earth with the most organic
patterns of skin.

Between the stretch marks, the wrinkles
the scars, cellulite & hair;
My, what a sight you would be.

What were you like before darkness?
Do you remember yourself in the light?

- conversations with myself

I sat up that night watching my heart unfold like an origami crane. The crane unfolded, a smile tucked into folds, into a map with glowing holes. I let my hands brush across the map, gently caressing the spots that were singed, burnt & ripped. I placed small kisses on my fingertips & let my hands fill the sections that no longer existed because of the damage. The funny thing about humanity is that we're all so broken but so consumed with accumulation & wealth that our hearts become emptier than our bank accounts & no one really seems to notice or care. I bet you if we stopped & focused on human healing the world would change so drastically that our future generations would genetically modify & glow from the inside out.

I wanted this so badly that my consciousness drifted into a dream state where the page reassembled into a smiling origami crane, scooped me unto its back & flew towards the majestic, gentle moon.

For a few hours during the night, I knew I would be safe.

- *paper cranes*

The most unconditional love
is that which forms between
the body & the mind.

To destroy itself casually,
& continue to survive
with each forgiving
breath.

- survival

One day, I promise you –
The cracks in your hands will erode into flowerpots & the fractures in your soul will become the very reasons to which you are regarded as the most beautiful miracle.

Vineyards of life will sprout from your calloused palms, & the world will kneel in admiration of your resurrection; tongues thirsty for the wines of your
weathered
love.

- tend to your garden

Didn't you know that your ego does not equate to your soul, love?

What hurts you right now
will not hurt you as much tomorrow.
No, it might not disappear into vapors (because that just isn't how our memories work), but you will indeed learn to live again.
& you will learn to love again.
So freely that even your lungs might learn how to breathe without your chest feeling far too constricted by the lump that has been lodged deep into the back of your throat, again.

One day you will open your eyes (& perhaps your heart) to the most wonderful realization that you are capable of far more than you have been settling for & you will. move. on.

Grow & let grow,
learn & let go.

No,
your ego does not equate to your soul, love.
& when that ego falls tired of its adrenaline rage, you will understand that it was your soul
that wanted
more.

- this is your conscience speaking

My beauty is not for you to quantify.
My beauty consists of many hopeful suns & tearful moons.
Each damaging & hopeful breath
producing the story that stands
before you.

I am the product of lovers
joined by fate
to deliver me from hatred.

Explore my spirit as it shifts through many faces
& believe that freedom
will one day
set us
free.

- I am more than my skin

Like floating grey clouds,
I will shift to make spaces
for light to shine through.

- mindful meditations

Leave daydreams in your wake.
Remind them of the rapid waves
that dance despite
the flooding.

- *be water*

There is no sense in depriving yourself of a fulfilled spirit.
People will enter your life with
no intention of nourishing your quality of living (& this is
only because they have been subconsciously programmed
to preserve freedom for their own). Do not wait for others to
defend what you deserve. Stand up for yourself & chase the
freedom your soul craves. The only real failure is giving up.

Do not disappoint yourself.

- soul food

You can't keep making wishes
upon starless chalkboard skies.
Set down your colours, darling
while we paint love with our eyes.

Sing along to every lullaby,
& banish all goodbyes
so we can rise up from the wreckage
to relearn how to fly.

- *watercolour waltz*

Release that which troubles you,
for a troubled heart confines the inspired mind.

Welcome in experience,
(both good & bad),
as cobble stones along the path of an enlightened self.

Express each emotion with gratitude
as these surges of existence solidify the presence of a
beating heart.

As long as this is true,
tomorrow will always promise the potential for
greatness.

- you are here

Let the places I don't belong expel me
& my receiving mind be resilient enough
to understand each reason
why.

- *moving on*

Take to the mountains
for your solemn solitude.
The clouds will console.

- headspace

Some people appear in your life only to inspire you.
Please loosen your grasp.

God sends us angels to temporarily inhabit human form to
teach us something when our ears are silent & our hearts
are dark.
Accept the experience.
Revel in its knowing arms,
& evolve.

Shed not a single tear that was not birthed out of gratitude.
When God finally calls that angel home & that person
returns to their true self, your lesson will be over.

Do not torment yourself over questioning why they have
changed, or what you had done to deserve the heartache
because you are
perfect.

You were perfectly in need of a message in the form of love.
Did you learn?

- healing pain with perspective

You can only get washed up
if you stop swimming.

- a reminder to artists

Let freedom remain
in the heart of an artist
surviving demise.

- create & live forever

Do not let opinions define your behavior.

Do not let statistics, facts or criticisms
be anything more than dirty words
to your ears.

Rise up to the occasion, creators
& fulfill your prophecies.

- church of he(art)

Understand the impact of your words.

Your mouth is armed with a powerful weapon containing the power to both heal & destroy.

How you choose to wield this weapon defines the type of person you are.

Be conscious.

- let love flow from your lips

Invite your demons
to our Sunday morning brunch.
Nothing loved can harm.

- peace is a state of mind

We are all kings & queens
birthed into one garden.
Adorn me in love,
& I shall worship thy earth.
Surrender your tears to the richness of soil
& rise up, anew
dressed in magic & mirth!

- existential conclusions

Soften the lines on your forehead, love.

Our days are too short numbered to
neglect the gentleness of
joy.

- daily reminders

Sometimes forgiving requires
peeling back the curtains each persisting dawn.
It means melting into
the gentle, warming sun.

I am a flower.
I must bloom towards the light.

- attention to intention

We laughed about our quarrels
& the pain dissolved to dust.
I guess it's true that all it takes
is patience, time & trust.

- *reconciliation*

Caterpillars molt
despite fear of unknown change
& so, too, shall I.

- trusting the process

If they threaten to leave, let them go.
Our wild hearts do not belong in captivity.

Wait for the one who will
make a home in your ribcage.

The one who will always fly home

& stay.

- the difference between love & lust is freedom

I've seen so many autumns with you.
So many seasons in which the
crisp, fall air would dry up my leaves
& strip me bare for a new beginning.

I've seen seasons last for years
& what seemed like years
dissolve like seasons...
But not with you.

With you the chill would spark flames.
Like a fire by the lake,
you were born of light;
warming the ground to heal,
illuminating our faces
to glow.

Like the birds in the sky,
you knew how & when to navigate
where & when you needed to
& always return home
when the cold subdued;
fueling the growing fires
lying dormant
between our
chests.

- sunset red & falling leaves

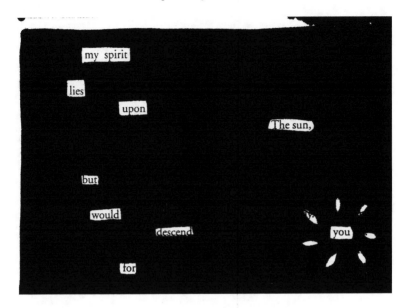

- my spirt lies upon the sun, but would descend for you

- resurrected into purpose

Kiss me until I realize how wrong I've been.
Until years melt into one single fragmented memory
dancing on the top of my tongue;
like honey & chocolate
& I can't.
get.
enough.

Kiss me until I question my expectations
& wonder how contemporary art might live
in a traditional world;
because that is what you are to me-
A moon in a sky of dark clouds.

Kiss me until I am new again;
like morning dew on freshly cut grass
& I can sink my fingers into the confines of the sky
reminding me of our gentleness.

Kiss me until we are free.

- it was you all along

I found myself questioning the intentions of my search.

Was it love that I longed for,
or redemption from the damage?

I learned the difference the day he came along & retired my façade.

From fog machines & strobe lights, I required no trickery to prove myself loveable this time.
No fancy embellishment to secure a spot within the warmest ventricle of his heart.

I watched him with a cautious eye as he scrubbed away my makeup, gently letting the sequins clink across the floor. "There you are..." he whispered into my neck, still damp from our ritual of freedom.

"... I've been looking for you."

- *unnecessary sequins*

I have been raised to believe that
salt water is the cure to all of life's problems;
the intention of sweat, the cleansing of tears,
the sounds of the sea.

But I have found the blue of home pooled within
each one of your eyes
yet you are the sweetest, saltless cure
to ever flow
across my lonely
lips.

- morning love letters

I am not an easy person to love.

There will be days where my neurological wiring might interfere with the essence of who
you know me to be. Coaxing & distorting the multi-colored layers of my complicated mind, I am a hostage to my own chemistry.

There may be days where I am unable to communicate the origin of my emotions,
but I cultivate experience with the conviction of a thousand burning suns.

I am not familiar with moderation or mediocrity.
Like a pendulum of sacred quartz, I will bridge the distance between us.
Suspend me by the devotion of your nourishing tongue.
Ignite my will to burn.

In happiness, I am a raging fire. In anguish, I am scattered ash.
Flames to dust, my mind is a forest fire.
Yet somehow, with you
I am free.

- heat, flames & confessions

I think he speaks to Angels
for I've watched his soul evolve.
How else might simple presence
prompt the shadows to dissolve?

How else might all the voices
rest their panicked heads to listen?
& even in the darkest storm
he somehow seems to glisten.

Some nights he tucks me in to sleep
with feathers in his hair.
My chaos stirs to silence,
leaving all my demons bare.

I'll bask in all his glory
to absorb his subtle hues.
Each time his tongue commands my name
I speak to Angels, too.

- *miracles in human form*

Sometimes loving is
a thing that heals me
accidentally.

- home remedies

I
love you
in ways that
force me
to
grow.

No one
deviates from
their comfort zones
without a
reason that's
worth
it.

- you are my reason for everything

I was a nomad before you.
Led by the soles of my diligent feet,
I would wander.

But you've gifted your vacancies to me.
Unravelling baggage you've made obsolete;

I am home.

- finding home

As surely as the sun does rise
so, too, will my soul reincarnate to find you.
Lifetime after lifetime
in all your forms.

By the guiding lights
in a sea of grey-
welcome me home.

Make me stay.

- northern lights

Thank you for finding
all of my insecurities
& loving them.

I didn't know
how to
before.

- love is a shaman worth trusting

When you are sad & your heart is heavy-
When your spirits have sunken low-
When your smile becomes less effortless-
When you've been wronged, misunderstood, disrespected-
When you are feeling lonely-
Love harder.

Match your pain with kindness, & then some.
Share your smile.
Stretch it out as far as you possibly can; like arms reaching
across the globe so far that they overlap & you find yourself
in your own embrace.

Give.
Not tangibly, but if you can – give tangibly too.
Love so hard that your face has no choice but to smile,
your heart has no choice but to swell,
your soul has no choice but to grow...

- *when all else fails*

April feels like December
Curled up by fireflies, below leaky rooftops
Night air is like oxygen
to the daydreamers touched by an
old poets
kiss.

Winter nights are like spring
with flowers blooming from just below my ribcage;
far below the shadowlands deprived of solar lips.

I am warm despite these shivers
crawling shyly down my spine
as they remind me, once again
that warmth exists only
where the fires
lie.

- where the fires lie

Drift closer, please.
Let me iron out the furrows in your brow with my fingertips.

I will retreat with you, silently. Straight into the depths of your caves to hang the very moon upon the strings of my retired marionettes when you crave nothing more than to surf upon the pinnacles of rumination.

I will remain here, willingly, to shine light upon your solitude from afar;
I will remain, patiently, to cloak you during those staggered breaths that always feel most shallow.

Stumble not, in your healing. Sink into yourself like a hot bath embellished with the essential oils of love. Inch by inch, the waters will rise against your skin welcoming you into peace.

Surrender to the knowing lead of your breath.
Remain gentle, when it's hard.
Sink further, & trust.
Drift closer, & awaken.

- let us share our healing

About the Author

Kristina Goltsis is a Greek-Canadian writer living in Mississauga, Ontario (Canada). An art lover with a variety of creative hobbies, Kristina has culminated her Hons. Psychology BA, Life Coaching Certification & 10 years of corporate experience into a personal pursuit for creative freedom. A poet, blogger, ghost writer, screenwriter, painter, photographer & writing coach – Kristina is constantly redefining herself through her art & discovering new ways to connect with the world.

Printed in the United States
By Bookmasters